Advanced Geordie Palaver

by

Scott Dobson

© 1993
ISBN 0 946928 43 6

First published by Frank Graham
Published by Butler Publishing 1993

BUTLER PUBLISHING
Thropton, Rothbury, NE65 7LP

Printed by Crescent Printing Company
195 Alexandra Road, Ashington, Northumberland NE63 9LA

INTRODUCTION

A THROBBING beat in the pulse of the night; the pounding of primeval poss-tubs; the eerie howl of the jungle whippet; the humming of the bumblers; the screech of the lops, tests the steadiest nerves among those intrepid explorers who journey into Darkest Geordieland. Today those adventurers can sally forth fore-armed with knowledge and experience – yet there are still those who – never return.

Some are stricken by the jungle fevers – the dreaded BEOR BILE or the SCREAMING SKITTERS, others fall victim to the CARNIVOROUS CUDDY or the PTERODACTYL PIGEON or even the MAN-EATING LEEK which spreads its evil fronds to tempt the unwary.

Yes, Geordieland is still a wild, untamed country where a man can journey deep among the trackless pitheaps and be seen no more – until perhaps years after a gibbering, mindless bearded wreck is found prone on the steps of the Prudhoe Street Betting shop moaning softly – FOWERBOBON ANSHIFTEDUBBLE.

Yet Geordieland beckons to the adventurer. It was to help such brave lads, aye. and lasses too that I wrote the first book in this series "Larn Yersel Geordie". I am greatly encouraged in my life's work by the kind suggestions of my faithful readers. Regrettably however, many were found impractical in the literary as well as the anatomical sense. Some of the most interesting were unprintable although the publisher and I have made enquiries among the Danish printing houses.

This particular book, however, *had* to be written (otherwise it would be a case of the dole clerk saying resignedly NOTYEAGYEN, an ancient Geordie blessing).

Besides as me grannie used to say: "wor bairns needs new byeuts". Yet Geordieland is beautiful. It is a wild, primitive beauty; for who has not been moved at the sight of the wattor of the Wear lapping peacefully round the netties and paanshops in the lovely lowlands of East Herrington? The people of Geordieland have an ancient culture all their own.

They have a natural kindness and courtesy which demands that they always say "Excuse me hinney" before they clag your lugs. There is one way, however, straight to their hearts. Speak their language and they will only clag one lug – and that but gently, with clarts. Take no notice of the wild tales which circulate in the planters and traders bars in such outpost settlements as North Kenton or Coxlodge. For instance, the current rumour that young Lord Tadger, one of the Shankhouse Tadgers whose scalp was found nailed to a netty lid at Throckley last month, had been done to death by that dreaded Geordie Secret Society – the MOGGIEMEN. This is just not true – for instance it was not Throckley but Bedlington and it was not his scalp but his right oxter. Besides, he was ever a feckless and arrogant young blade as well as being a Sunderland supporter. I do beseech you, however, dear reader – *do* learn the Geordie language.

Pay the Geordie native the compliment of learning his language and he will cherish you. I have seen myself grim-faced AADGAJEEZ (elders of the tribe) cry with emotion to hear a visitor speak a few words of broken Geordie, "What a canny fella" they murmured as they brayed him inter the grund.

Essential reading

Larn Yersel' Geordie by Scott Dobson. Written with the intention of making you a fluent speaker of geordie.

Geordie Words and Phrases by George Todd. Pages of useful phrases (and translations) to help you communicate on Tyneside.

The Geordie Dictionary by Frank Graham. Essential.

GANONKIDDA — GITSTUCKIN !

OFFICIAL HANDBOOK TO THE
GEORDIE LANGUAGE

THIS BOOK is now the official handbook to the armed forces of Geordieland and is personally endorsed in that capacity by Field Marshal St. James Park, N.C.B. (and bar), General Officer Commanding the Geordieland Army. All the regiments mentioned below have interpreters trained by myself. The Scotswood Guards; The Elswick Sikhs; The Rye Hill Assault and Battery R.A.; McKeag's Horse; the Corbridge Camel Corps; the Guide Post Gurkhas; the Osborne Road Women's Voluntary Corps; the Grindon Grenadiers; the Mitford Marine Corps; the High Spen Hussars; the Consett Cossacks; the Longbenton Lancers; the Framwellgate Moor Foreign Legion; the Sacriston Sappers and Miners and the Newcastle University Special Hair Service. It is

The Scotswood Guards

also most important that civilians own a copy, too, especially those who serve in the following capacity: District Commissioners, hot-dog barrow service engineers; corporation midden men; quantity surveyors in the State Stotty Cake factories; Cox'ns of the Blackhill and Consett lifeboats; pilots of the Shankhouse Ship Canal; foremen in the Berwick on Tweed Clarts Quarries; and itinerant black pudding and fish finger salesmen.

This book may also be used by students who wish to take 'O' and 'A' levels in Geordie language, and what is more, this is required reading for those taking their B.A. (Geordie). The degree course is held at the University of Holy Island under the direction of Professor G. Bashmoodie.

Stop-press

The publisher and I are proud to report that His Serene Highness Prince Wornedz Nowtbutcanny II, hereditary ruler of Geordieland has been pleased to confer upon us his Royal Appointment. Below is his Royal Seal of Approval issued from the Palace of Jarra Slax.

THE USE OF GEORDIE

IT SHOULD be understood that although many Geordies speak English (indeed a variant of that language is taught in the reservation mission schools) it is considered unpatriotic and insulting to the spirits of the Geordie forefathers to use any other tongue but Geordie in intimate tribal ceremonies.

There actually exists in the deep Geordie jungle a number of intensely nationalistic and patriotic organisations who keep the flame of Pan-Geordieism eternally burning. *In dealing with these bodies Geordie must always be used.* Speak to them in English and they will don the flat cap and muffler of war – break the tab-end of peace and, brandishing their KWARTA-HAMMERZ take to the war-path and borst yer gobs. Here is a list of these fanatical organisations for your information while travelling in the tribal heartlands.

Always speak Geordie to the following bodies:

Officials and members of
{ Any COONZIL (an elected governing body).
Any SOSHALKLUB (a recreative body).
Any BOOZAH (a government rest-bungalow).

The following specific organisations:

The Blaydon and District Bolshevik Jolly Boys and Leek Conservancy Society;

The West Sleekburn Numismatic and Greyhound Coursing Old Comrades Democratic and Bingo Club;

The Red Row Sons and Daughters of the Industrial Revolution;

The Pickled Tripe and Stotty Cake Appreciation Society of Tyne Dock;

The Blackhall Colliery Over-sixties Karate Club;

The Esh Winning Country Dancing and Old-Age Pensioners Sky-diving Society;

The Shincliffe Retired Gentlewomen's Association for the encouragement of the Arts and All-in Wrestling;

The Birtley Townswomen's Guild Jam-making and Black Panther Society;

The Seghill Senior Citizens Rose, Sweet-pea and Samurai Swordmanship Society.

IT IS NOT ENOUGH MERELY TO SPEAK GEORDIE.

One must also know and use the correct forms of greeting.

Proceed in the following manner:

The organisation or its representative must be saluted with the *whole of the right hand displayed open.* This shows that no weapons are carried. Make sure that *all* the fingers are extended. Do not make the near-fatal error, as did a visiting Wolf-cub Commissioner some years ago and salute with two fingers. This was immediately misunderstood and before the elders of the tribe could intervene, fanatical young Geordie braves had clagged his lug.

The salute having been given – then the first greeting is made.

Phrase A. "WATFETTLETHEDAYLADZ"

The congregation will reply –

Phrase B. "NOWTBUTCANNY HOOZYERSEL"

The next greeting from the visitor will be –

Phrase C. "BYTHATSA BONNY GANZEE YORLASSIS KNITYER"

The congregation will reply –

Phrase D. "GIVOWER SHEGORRIT ONASTOREKLUB"

The visitor will then ask –

Phrase E. "YELLBETEKIN AGILL WIVUZ?"

The ceremony will wind up with –

Phrase F. "DIVVENTMIND IFWEDEELIKE"

All present will then smack their lips and say –

Phrase G. "YEBUGGARMAR' ".

It is useful at this stage to understand not only the words but the deeper meaning of this ceremony. It begins with a greeting (phrase A) then a counter-greeting (phrase B). Phrase C compliments the tribesmen on their gorgeous apparel – phrase D is self-deprecating. Phrase E is an offer of refreshment, phrase F an acknowledgement of acceptance and phrase G is the most popular Geordie benediction and blessing. Phrase G is peculiar to Geordieland and although sounding more like an insult than a benediction it really approximates to the English "My dear chap"; the French "Cher Monsieur"; the German "Mein leiber Herr"; the Russian "Gospodin" or the Indian "Salaam Sahib". So – remember that phrase G (to recapitulate, YEBUGGER-MAR') is of great use to the Geordie linguist and will ensure your being well received in Geordieland under all circumstances, even those as far apart in general nature as, say, an introduction to the Bishop of Durham or an attempt to get into Grey's Club, Newcastle, without a tie on. So now, dear reader, you are beginning to appreciate the true subtleties of advanced Geordie and will be able to, in reasonable safety, visit the very heartlands of the Geordie tribes. You may even walk up Scrogg Road, Walker and greet the warriors of the WAALKERLADZ tribe thus. HOOYEGANONLADZ – MINDTHEMZ BONNYGALLUSES

The Waalkerladz Tribe

YEGORRON. You will also, to your delight, be able to understand the roars of abuse that are hurled back at you.

Pronunciation for the advanced student

In the original "Larn Yersel' Geordie" you will remember that some trouble was taken to instruct readers in the production of the Geordie 'R'. All that was, of course, merely an introduction to that vital skill.

To reach the advanced level of pronunciation one must use advanced methods. The first book suggested painting the tonsils with a compound of surgical spirit and Madras Curry Powder to achieve a typical raucous Geordie 'R'. Such mild and elementary treatments must now be set aside in favour of the more robust approach suitable for the advanced student.

The advanced aid to this necessary pronunciation is called the 'FLAMBEAU' method and is invaluable for the conditioning of the tonsil. The surface of the tonsil must be rendered abrasive so that the 'R' will reverberate in a specific manner. The Geordie Poet Laureate, Lord Pitpownie, puts it rather well in his "Ode to a heather-clad slagheap". In the section devoted to the gambolling of the gallowa's he wrote:

" with the soond, the roond soond, of a cantering canny cuddy coughin' up a clarty cloot".

This is exactly the sort of sound we require. The 'flambeau' method will attain it for you.

Instructions for the use of the 'FLAMBEAU' method in producing a Geordie 'R'

You will need the following items:

> One crate of Brown Ale
>
> One pint of methylated spirits
> Mixed with –
> One pint of high-octane petrol
>
> One fuse
>
> One box of matches
>
> One telephone
>
> Unbounded courage.

The meaning of the term 'FLAMBEAU'

Perhaps you have seen waiters preparing dishes over a spirit stove in one of those intimate little transport caffs in the old quarter of Spennymoor or Backworth. Perhaps you have seen them using the flaming liquid or spirit in the little pan (and making a flaming mess of it). That is identical to the 'flambeau' method which you will apply to your *tonsils*.

How to do it

1. First, the pre-medication:
   Drink the contents of the crate of Brown Ale on an empty stomach or sitting in a chair.

2. When suitably PALATIK (which means in English 'lubricated') drink the cocktail of spirits and petrol, but *do not swallow* – gargle it in the throat.

3. Shove the fuse up your left nostril until it makes contact with the gargling fluid.

4. Light the blue touchpaper and retire to a safe distance.

The result of this activity will be an initial intense desire to ring 999 on the telephone. This is to be expected, but do decide *in advance* whether you need police, fire brigade or ambulance or all three. The grilling action of the 'flambeau' method is most efficacious and you will find to your delight that the tonsils have been rendered to a medium rare condition which will have you saying 'R' frequently and accurately. In fact it is not unknown for practitioners to go on repeating 'R' for twelve hours in the sheer joy of attainment. Now once the fire brigade has gone back to the station and you have been damped down – try your new sound by repeating this practice sentence (avoiding of course such decadent south-country public school exclamations like "Grooogh" or "Yarrooh" while practising. Keep a stiff upper tonsil).

The practice sentence is – "Aroond Rothbary and Rowlands Gill the rugged rocks gan clittor clatter doon the brae and through the watter".

After you have been damped down . . .

Every 'R' must be clearly enunciated – for example – RRRRothbaRRRRy and "clittoRRRR". Odd bits of dislodged tonsil should be hoyed aback o' the fire.

There is, however, a simplified method for those who may find the 'flambeau' method too rigorous. This is Eastern in origin and is called "The tonsil ceremony". I am here under an obligation to the executors of the late noted Japanese author, Mr. Heykidda Hoyahammerowerheor. In his learned treatise "Larn yersel' Hari-Kiri" this retired Kamikaze pilot refers to the practice of trimming the tonsils with an ancestral corn-cutter. This method will obviously have a certain attraction to those who interest themselves in Zen or go to night schools for flower arrangement. It does, admittedly, have a fragrant sense of the mysterious East.

In dealing with the Geordies one must be able to recognise the representatives of their tribal hierarchy

It is of course pointless to be able to speak the language without being able to recognise at a glance those particular natives whose social position requires that Geordie should be always used in social intercourse. In the matter of tribal customs, by the way, who knows but that you may be accorded the honour of becoming the "broon ale" brother of a native chief. This is not unknown and if you keep practising you may well qualify for such an honour, which entitles you to wear native dress and buy the beer for your sponsor.

A particular sub-section of the united tribes of Geordieland are the 'pigeon-priests'. These are elders whose lives are devoted to the care, upbringing and exercise of the holy fowls of the Geordie nation – the racing pigeons. The costume of the pigeon-priests is ancient and colourful. First they may be recognised by the large medallion worn round the neck. (It is not actually a

The pigeon-priests

medallion but a pigeon-clock). They are invariably attended by acolytes bearing large rectangular baskets of native manufacture and large sacks of pigeon-corn. Both priests and acolytes carry their heads in a peculiar upward-looking manner at all times and wear shin-pads as they continually fall over things – so enwrapt are they in contemplation of heaven. At all times too they utter continual shrill whistles and objurgations which are prayers to the pigeon-gods.

Their temples are called 'KREEZ' or 'DUKITZ' and may be recognised by their siting, generally near railway lines. Another recognition feature of these temples is the colour, which for some inexplicable reason matches that of whichever ship is being built in the area. The chief pigeon-priests – the equivalent of Christian Cardinals, Grand Muftis, Gurus or Moderators have a special dress, This consists of a large flat cap of dark cloth spotted with a mysterious white-spattered pattern, a muffler of white samite, mystic, wonderful and a large gold watch-chain. From the chain dangles medals of precious metals decorated with pigeon motifs. The number of medals testify to the sanctity and mystic professional ability of the wearers. A special diet of broon ale and stotty cake develops a generous paunch which serves to display the medals to perfection and as the chief-priest walks along the jewellery tinkles like temple bells. The most distinctive part of the dress, however, is the boots or BYEUTZ of special pattern. To obtain a particular hue, patina, scent and texture they are daily immersed in pigeon guano which imparts to them a particular charm. Most of these chief-priests are bachelors, divorced men or separated. This is not so much an exercise of holy celibacy as an occupational risk. In fact one could truly say that the only birds they fancy are pigeons. To demonstrate this attitude we may refer to the ancient folklore of these people where a tale is told of a pigeon-fancier in the reign of King Worfred (AD 1341-1400). This worthy man was waiting up at his allotment, standing by the pigeon-temple and waiting for a race to come in, pigeon-clock at the ready. His acolyte was there too, preparing a tasty dish of pigeon corn chow mein. Down the road a funeral passed by. The chief priest solemnly raised his flat cap. Salaaming deeply, his acolyte said, "Hey Ned, aa dident knaa ye wor se respectful-like te funerals". "Whey man", said the chief priest, "Ye gorra show sum respect te the wife". The

The Geordie Cat

pigeon-priests have, however, one strong tribal "tabu". Cats. They hate, detest, abominate and will assassinate at all times the feline race. Cat safaris are held regularly in all pigeon-worshipping tribal reservations and many a horny-handed pitman who will spend his leisure carving little wooden crutches for pigeons with bunions or gout will mercilessly hunt the local moggies on foot armed only with a KWARTAHAMMA. Evolution has taken a hand in the development and bodily structure of the Geordie cat in consequence, and the local breeds are now born with little steel shrapnel helmets and equipped with overdrive in the back legs.

The Whippet-priests

These men look rather like the pigeon-priests. It is their actions which mark them firmly as whippet-priests rather than their apparel. For instance if they see a new baby in the pram they do not chuck it under the chin or make goo-goo noises. They invariably feel its nose and slap its flanks before offering it a dog-biscuit. Their chief point of recognition is a large bone displayed in the breast pocket and a pound of stewed tripe carried in the watch-fob. Their charges are intelligent animals. Warmly clad in mohair hand-tailored two-piece battledress with little gumboots in the winter, they have been known to reject beer with floaters in it and bite the barman forebye.

Now we come to the most exotic cult of all, the leek-priests
The leek-priest's life is entirely given up to the worship of this noble vegetable. A special part of the leek-priest's costume is the decorative (and functional) cords tied round the trousers. This is to prevent the leek-manure from soiling his LANGLININZ or John L's. He is rarely divorced or separated from his wife, being so steeped in leek-lore puts him in a continual sort of trance, and bringing him before a matrimonial court is an arrant waste of time. Indeed a recent case heard at Dinnington amplifies this point.

So conditioned were the defendant's mental processes that anything unconnected with leeks was immediately filtered out. Consequently, when the wife's lawyer asked him, "Is it not true that you constantly neglected your wife?" the leek-fancier answered, "Aa waddent dream o' neglectin' hor, whey aa useter put new rabbit-muck in hor bed ivvory day and she got a reglar drink o' broon ale and pig's blood afore aa settled hor doon fer the neet". He nearly got divorced for cruelty until the court realised he was speaking not of his wife, but of his prize leek. Because of marauders and leek-assassins, he is generally armed with a sawn-off shotgun and a brace of bazookas. He always carries a large roll of insulating tape round his neck to repair the high-voltage wire round his leek-bed. The upper-income leek-priests, they who have won many prizes, have been known to build concrete strongpoints around the allotments and to cross-breed jaguars with the domestic whippets thus to guard the safety of the leek enclave and its precious contents.

A note about the particular traditional posture of the priest-people of all denominations
All pigeon-priests, whippet-priests or leek-priests have a peculiar posture which they invariably adopt known as

HUNKERSITTIN. This is employed for rest or transcendental meditation. It is the mark of the true Geordie guru; the Masai may stand on one leg, the Red Indian may prefer to cross the legs, the African to sit on a wooden stool, the Yoga practitioner balance on his left oxter, but the Geordie will always "sit on his hunkers". It is thought that this position originates from the shortage of arm-chairs in the rest-lounges down the coal-pits.

Finally let us deal with the two types of fundamental head-gear that you will see worn in Geordieland

Naturally we deal first with the cloth cap. Many misguided patriots would like to see this go; "destroy the cloth-cap image" they say.

As the Hanoverian dynasty dealt with the kilt of our brothers in Scotland, so would the Southern oppressors like to deal with our national dress. There is, too, a Fifth Column working within. Countless ambitious Geordie wives under the dread influence of television would like to see their men in Homburgs or Guardee bowlers with narrow brims or even rakish Dickensian caps of the type affected by pop musicians. In executive enclaves like Washington and Killingworth New Towns or the purlieus of Darras Hall or High West Jesmond, there are strong pressure groups at those sort of coffee mornings where the guests call each other 'darling' instead of 'hinny' and all the loos have mink netty-cosies on them. This has led to an inevitable reaction and it is reported that the ancient Geordie custom of CLASHIN-WORLASS is being revived. The cap is not so much a cap but a way of life to the true full-blooded Geordie. Concealed in its ample folds he may keep his "bait" for the pit, the corn for his pigeons and the small parcels of rabbit-manure wrapped in whippet-skin for his leeks. In short this slack, capacious and often floppy headgear is in reality a most functional article. As a well-known AADGADJEE of a famous Geordie tribe said to me the other day, "Whey man, ye cuddent git mair than two oonces o' the stoat's droppins ah use fer me leeks intiv the croon o' one o' them fond wee hats".

The Dut

This term, of peculiar and archaic beauty refers to the bowler hat. Sometimes the word 'bowler' is pronounced phonetically,

thus "bowel-er", rather than "bohler" in the Southern manner. The Geordie 'dut' or 'bowel-er' bears little resemblance to the stock-exchange or Guardee variant affected principally in the City of Westminster or by Mr. Steed of the 'Avengers'. It has a capacious dome to it and a wider brim and is always worn either one size too large or one too small. Dut-wearers off-duty, as it were, can therefore be identified by bent ears or deep grooves over the eyebrows.

The 'dut' is a ceremonial headdress, being worn by ordinary tribal Geordies at weddings, christenings and funerals or even Store Dividend days (in the areas where that ancient festival still prevails). It is worn, however, at all times by the petty chiefs or GAFFERZ of the shipyards and factories. Even some Geordie undertakers in reservations such as Easington prefer it to the top-hat, having naturally no wish to be mistaken for an exiled coal-owner on holiday.

The foot-gear of Geordieland

These are known by the native expression of 'GREET-TAGGERTY BYEUTZ' or more simply 'WORKBYEUTZ' or 'NARLEYGREETBYEUTZ'. They are eminently suitable for such national customs as HOWKINCOAL or WAAKIN TEWORK ATWAALKOR. They are pigeon-muck proof, broon-ale proof and one can use them to plodge across the five rivers. During the recent war in Europe, patriotic Geordies gave their WORKBYEUTZ to the nation and they were used, filled with concrete to anchor the platforms of the Mulberry Harbours on

Byeutdansin

'D'-Day' They are also still today used in the traditional
BYEUTDANSIN to the tune of "Keep yer feet still Geordie
Hinny" carried out on coronations or the occasion of opening
new WORKINMENSKLUBS.

The most famous practitioner of BYEUTDANSIN is Mr.
William (Big Bill) Barrass of Byker. This, by the way, is an
ancient Geordie sur-name probably meaning that the bearer of
it wore a whippet-skin kilt – 'Barrass' can be roughly translated as
'trouserless'. His dynamic series of bangs and crashes amplified
by being performed upon an upturned herring box have been
compared to the walk-off drum solos of such percussive practitioners as Gene Krupa and Buddy Rich. In his young days he
danced with Pavlova and it is reported that she was so overcome
by his enormous natural talent that she swooned.

However, Mr. Barrass's detractors have since put it about
that this was caused by his standing on her toe. Readers must
make up their own minds here as Mr. Barrass is six foot three
in height and weighs twenty-two stones.

Now let us consider pronunciation again.

Variants of the Geordie Language

If we accept that the overlordship of the Geordie nation runs
from the Tweed roughly to the Tees, north to south, then we will
find many variants of the language within that area. Sometimes it
changes dramatically inside the distance of but a few miles. The
further south for instance, the softer the 'R'. Beginners therefore
in Geordie tend to confine their early efforts in speech to south
Durham.

No major tonsil modification is needed for practitioners in
this area. Also the 'ye' or 'ee' (you) of the north changes subtly
to the 'thee' or 'thoo' of the south. In my early days as a regimental
interpreter during the famous World punch-up of 1939-45 it was
my duty, in a Geordie regiment, to tell the officers what the men
were saying and vice-versa. This was very necessary otherwise we
would have lost the war. Take the case of one young subaltern
from Bournemouth who gallantly charged a NAAFI queue single-
handed under the mistaken impression that these harmless Other
Ranks were members of the Waffen S.S. (Leibstandarte Adolf
Hitler).

It took all my powers of persuasion and a full company of the Redcaps to hold him off while it was explained that they were actually Geordie allies of the British army and were singing "Blaydon Races" and not "We march against England". The first time that I had to execute my office was when a large gun became lodged in a Northumbrian dunghill. The captain was sent for and stood beating his legs with one of those little sticks officers carry for that purpose. "Ay say," he finally enquired of me, "Doo you think thyet a horse cood pool it oot." I translated to the farmer. "Whey man," said the farmer, "Ye canna put a cuddy in theor, it's ower heavy – ye'd hing the bugger – ye'd stoppits breeth." The captain was so impressed by my rapid translation – "He does not recommend that course of action, sir", that he made me a bombardier on the spot. I was further promoted when I averted a mutiny among some Welsh gunners attached to us. Misunderstanding the orders of a lance-sergeant from Pelton Fell, they turned right instead of left. "Noo lookstha

"*Ye canna put a cuddy in theor!*"

heyuh" said the lance-sergeant, "Ha's the Hen Ce Ho and when ha gives a horder it'll be hobeyed." Apparently this must have sounded like something rude in Welsh because they poised themselves to fill him in. For averting that fracas I became a staff-sergeant.

I was later commissioned in the field for meritorious conduct in explaining to a militia intake from Devon and Cornwall exactly what a 'COOKOOSE' was. Prior to that the poor lads had wandered about starving unable to locate where their rations were lodged.

A Special South-Geordie Custom

In the south of Geordieland, near to the Teesside badlands, there is the custom of the 'touch', which sounds rather erotic. However, it merely implies the addition of a small amount of lemonade to a pint of beer. Hardened club-members from Ashington have been known to swoon at the thought of such alcoholic heresy.

However – the Geordie is nothing if not tolerant of the foibles of his brother tribesmen and in cases like this he contents himself with a quiet comment such as "THEWANTPUTTIN-DOON". Now, to fully understand the Geordie it is necessary to know something of the history of the tribes.

The Geordies have a long and proud history

Quoting the titles and the deeds of these tribal notables will endear you to the most militant Geordie brave. First of course in this long list of worthies is Arthur Leonard Edward Brown (or BROON) who invented the famous Geordie beverage of that name.

Having prepared the first recorded brew he was stuck for a name for it. Seeking inspiration he knocked back fifteen bottles and was breathalised as he sped home on his chariot drawn by five spirited whippets. "What the' caall 'ee?" said the POLISS or tribal policeman. "BRZZOOON", said Arthur, who was, of course, PALATIK. "Eh," said the POLISS. "BROON" said Arthur, pulling himself together. The POLISS wrote this down, moistening his pigeon-bone ball-pen. "Initials?" said the POLISS.

"What the' caall 'ee?"

"A.L.E.", said Arthur. "By – yons a fond nyem – BROON A.L.E.", said the POLISS. At that point Arthur panned the POLISS and shouted "Eureka! – that's what aall caall it – Broon Ale".

Understandably, King Worporcy III, the reigning monarch of Geordieland, gave him a Royal Pardon later, and the beverage was officially named "Broon Ale".

Such a benefactor to the Geordie nation was naturally given a peerage and became Baron Broon of Burradon Toon. When he died he was given a State funeral with a ham tea and buried in Backworth Cathedral. Above his tomb is carved the words: "Gone to the great brewery in the sky".

In the realm of Fine Art we have Thomas Bewick, the father of wood-engraving who began life carving rude words on the netty door at Cherryburn where he lived. "Aa mind me fethor copped us", he wrote in his memoirs – "aah rued it aal reet when he kicked me hint end". He got a job drawing for the "Blaydon Courier" but, never progressing beyond drawing the names out of the hat for the machine-room weekly raffle; he fell into bad company and joined the Northern Arts Association. After his "Chillingham Bull" was refused by the Friends of the Laing Art Gallery on grounds of obscenity he took to Town Planning and was responsible for the design of Bewick-on-Tweed.

Lord Armstrong founded the firm of Armstrongs (known in Geordie as DOONAT THUFAKTRY). Graduating in the arms industry from simple catapults made from his grannie's bloomer elastic, he eventually invented the rifled gun. Well – he didn't actually invent it. Seeing one lying about unattended at Fenham barracks one day he just naturally rifled it, together with three dozen shells from the armoury and transported them down to Scotswood Road in a cart drawn by sixteen strong whippets before the barracks commander noticed it had gone or the law twigged on like.

George Stephenson was, of course, a great folk hero – inventing the railway engine. In point of fact, like all great inven-

tions, it came about by accident. He was working as a road man with Longbenton Council (the pit being idle) and suddenly wondered what would happen if he put a tar-boiler on rails. Before he knew what happened he was down at King's Cross and being cheered in by the General Secretary of the National Union of Railwaymen, which organisation had been hastily formed when they heard about George's tar-boiler on the six o'clock news.

Cuthbert Collingwood was, of course, Nelson's chief checky at Trafalgar and was first into action on the day of the battle, full of hell, having heard that Real Madrid had been all called up for the Spanish Navy. This was only natural – him being a strong Newcastle United supporter. After the battle he took all these Spanish lads prisoner and flogged them for ransom to Sunderland Football Club. Now you know why Sunderland has been so unfortunate – those lads must be on average about 185 years old now. No wonder the forward line is a bit slow off the mark.

Last, but by no means least, there is the Emperor Hadrian, the famous Roman disc-jockey who later settled in Geordieland after doing his national service with the Blaydon Bersaglieri. He married a Blakelaa lass and bought a house in Darras Hall which he called 'Pons Aelius' in memory of his rather effeminate company commander. Eventually he confided in their lass that he was missing the dolce vita – the sweet life that he had known back home in Rome in his young days. Whereupon their Bella suggested that they should build a club and call it that. "This Darras Haall Workin' Men's club is ne good," said Bella. "Aam deed chowked off wi' aall them foisty pies, beers full o' floaters and man – the torns is aaful!"

"By yebuggar wor Bella hinny, canny woman," said the Emperor. "We'll build "La Dolce Vita"; that'll myek thor gansies shoot up thor backs like venetian blinds". And they did too. There was a gadjee called Nero did the cabarets with his two performing lions (and a bucket of water) – they had "Quo Vadis on Ice" and a personal appearance in his gladiator's claa-hammer coat by Victor Manure. However, there was all this trouble with the Sewage Canal and the supply of Indian snake-charmers ran out. So they flogged the club. He couldn't put a foot wrong, that Hadrian. Two buyers were fighting each other to get control.

Eventually a Mr. Barnum got the performing lions and the snake-charmers. The club went to the Baileys.

There are many more great Geordies but this book is really intended to give a general background to Geordie culture. For those of you with historical interests we can do no more than recommend you to read the "History o' the Geordies" which, after years of patient research should be on your bookstalls shortly.

Now let us turn to tribal songs.

The tribal songs of the Geordies

The first Geordie songs were war-songs.

(Of course thor wors, ye fond gonniel, whe elses wad the' be?
Editor.)

Perhaps I'd better put that in a different way – the first Geordie songs were martial songs.

(Marshal had nowt te de wi' them – me aad grandfethor useter sing thim lang afore Marshal wes born.—Editor.)

The first Geordie songs were warriors' chants used in battle such as: "Bray – bray – braythebuggers" or "O God of battles, borst thor gobs". Later more peaceful ballads such as "Geordie haad the bairn", "Blaydon Races" and "The Paan-shop bleezin' " reflected a more settled period in Geordie music. There were, too, the protest songs such as "Blow the wind southerly", sung originally by council house tenants living to the north of Walker Bone Yard. "Oh don't deceive me" was written by a member of the Jesmond Residents Association during the discussion on the route of the new motorway and "Waters of Tyne" was personally directed at the mismanagement of the bar by the steward of Tadgers Main Social Club. Here are two, however, which have never before been published. I recorded them at a social evening and pie and pea supper held by the Low Fell Jacobin, Nihilist, Primitive Bolshevist Conservative and Unionist Quoits league for the sons and daughters of ruptured Twist Dancers (to which is affiliated the Windy Nook Townswomen's Guild Home Bootlegging and Bunny Club). It's a little thing which goes something like this –

Lament for a Drunken Son

O where hae ye been, my son, my son?
O where hae ye been, ma bonny young Will?
Aa've been te the club, Aa cud de wi' a sub
For Aa'm bad wi' the beor and Aa've had me fill.

Where gat ye yor beor, my son, my son?
Where gat ye yor beor, ma bonny young Will?
Aah gorrit at Carters, its rotted me garters
And Aa've boozed me way up and doon Westgate Hill.

What gat ye for beor, my son, my son?
What gat ye for beor, hast been on the broon?
Aa've had broon, Aa had ambers in the back bar at Balmbras,
Aa'm weary o' boozin' and fain would lie doon.

What became o'your money, my son, my son?
What became o' your money, ma bonny bit gem?
Aa spent it on lasses and glasses o' Basses,
Aa'm weary o' boozin' and Aa think Aa'll stay hyem.

And finally a love-song from the Middle Ages of Geordieland when chivalry flowered:

Lady Gortie o' Byker

By Byker tower sweet Ouseburn's stream
Runs bickerin' to the Tyne.
Wiv aal the breezes o' the morn
The weshin's dryin' fine.

There's joy in Byker's bonny tower
There's morth within the hall,
But doon the cheek o' Lady Gortie
The tricklin' tear-drops fall.

She sits upon the scullery bench
Hor cousins by hor side.
Yet loath is she te don the dress
That's fittin' for a bride.

Howway – Lord Backworth's on his way
Ye hae ne time to spare.
So get the mud-pack off yer fyece
And the corlers oot yer hair.

Of aal the Byker lasses
She wes the greatest swell.
Wi' lace upon hor nylon draas,
The finest that Parrishes sell.

A Woolworths necklace she'd put by
And plastic earrings gay.
And the bonniest see-through ganzie
For this hor weddin' day.

O Bella wud ye think it hard,
Te wed against yer will.
Aa nivvor loved Lord Backworth yet
Aa divvent like him still.

Ye knaa Lord Backworth tuk us oot
Te Billy Botto's Club.
But he was ower fat for me
He's got a belly like a tub.

But he has got me da's consent,
Wor muthor's storn command.
But aa'm in luv wi' a thin young lad
Who'll cum and claim me hand.

O Bella softly list te me,
Aa still may 'scape the snare,
This morn aa sent te Wallsend Club
Bowld Archie will be theor.

So hurry on bowld Archie,
On yer psychedelic scooter
There's nane in all Northumberland
Such a gay romantic suitor.

Ay well aa ken his heart is true
He will, he must be here
He'll be up and ower wor backyard waall
Tho' rotten wi' the beor.

Far is the way, the tram-lines deep
The breadth o' Shields Road wide
Whey, Gortie 'ere yer true love comes
Ye'll be Lord Backworth's bride.

Wi' stately solemn step the vicar
Climbs up the backyard stair.
Alas, alas where's Archie?
He'll nivvor make it there.

Luk oot, cum bye Lord Backworth's here
Ye hev nae time te flee.
O hasten hurry Archie bowld
Ye useless-lookin' bee.

Bowld Archie

In hor Homestores goon she wadn't dress
Nor hor jewels of marvellous wealth
Ne whippet-skin shoes, ne nylon stays
Nor hor teeth from the National Health.

O Bella hoy the winder up
Let in the air ter me,
Look doon inter wor backyard.
And tell us what ye see.

Yor fethor's standin' on the step
Yor muthor's at the coalhoose door.
And doon the backlane aall the guests
Lord Backworth rides before.

Haad yer gob – a scooter's soond.
It soondeth faint but clear
Whey luk we's climbed on the netty roof
Bowld Archie has got heor.

And up deed quick got Gortie
Nee ailment had she mair.
She nigh on sprained her oxter
As she dashed doon the backyard stair.

She sprang amang the clothes props
And through the weshin' flew
Until she reached Bowld Archie's side
Hor breath she scarcely drew.

Lord Backworth nipped up to see the bride
Up tiv hor room alone.
He corsed and swore and kicked the cat
For the bonnie bride had blown.

Sair did hor fethor de his nut,
Hor muthor hor baalgoon did rend.
But Gortie's off wi' Archibald
Te the club at bonny Wallsend.

VOCABULARY OF GEORDIE PHRASES

G for Geordie   *E for English*

G.   ### E.

At the Works Dance

Ye'll knaa the cheefchecky?   May I introduce the Managing
                                         Director?

Thatzabonny baalgoon   What a stunning dress your
yorlassis gorron.   good lady is wearing.

Ganon heva gargle.   Champers?

Yehevvin atab kidda?   Care for a king-size dear lady?

Fancy a bit prance abootlike?   May I have this dance, assum-
                                         ing that you are free of
                                         course?

Ye been i'this gaffafore?   Do you come here often?

Ownly whenthuh barschuckoot.   Only during the mating season.

Canwewaalk yeheyem?   May I escort you home?

Hooaboot yeanme   Would you care to dine with
gantethebingo?   me at my club?

Howwaydoon tuthe chippy.   Fancy a late snack?

Ahfancytekkinhor   By Jove, I'd like to show that
abackathgasworks.   girl my etchings.

Yegotnehyems togante?   And that concludes the even-
                                         ing's entertainment.

The Union Meeting

Shutyorgobs.   Silence please for the secre-
                                         tary's report.

Haadon - givower!   On a point of order.

Themfor and themagyen.   Assents and dissents please.

Seeyezaal doonith'bar.   May I declare the meeting
                                         closed?

G.	**E.**

In the Doctor's Waiting Room

Heyuhord abootwor Meggiesbadleg?	My maternal Aunt Margaret is incapacitated. Alas she cannot walk without assistance.
Worbairns gothuh skitterzagyen.	My little son is having trouble with his digestive tract.
Worbellaz in theclub agyen.	My cousin Isabella is anticipating a happy event.
Wormans badwi thebeor.	My husband has been overdoing it lately, I fear.
Ahdeenowt butbowk.	I do so suffer with my stomach.
Canye gizan eatinbottle forwor man?	I wonder Doctor if you could prescribe some compound to promote my husband's appetite?
Shezbeenunder thedoctor wi'thebile.	Mother has been in the hands of the medical authorities due to a general condition of debility.
Ittukim aalday temekasample.	Father is suffering from stricture.
Omebellysbad.	This indigestion is most distressing.

At School

(*Morning assembly*).

Eyes doon lukkin.	Now a prayer.
Ifah findthelad that braydthewinder inaal brayhim.	Vandalism is sinful.

(*Physical education*).

Whenahsez lowp yelowps.	On the word go – all jump as high as you can.
Divvenborstthebaal yefondgonniel.	You must learn to treat the equipment with care.

G.	E.
Art and Craft Lesson	
Ganon clagiton.	Now I want you all to carefully glue this in place.
Weshoot yerboodie.	Will the class wash out the paintpots and make them nice and clean.
Mindyorclarty.	Tut, tut – you are an untidy painter.
Ifacatch thelad wotshoyin wattor aalchashim.	It is against the school rules to discharge water at your neighbour.
Divvent clash yerdesklids se.	Please close your desks quietly.
Armed Forces	
Cookoose.	Building under the administration of the Catering Corps.
Langlininz.	Army issue winter underpants.
Workornel.	The Commanding Officer.
Heyup.	Take cover!
Lowse yer gullies.	Unfix bayonets.
Clagyergullieson.	Fix bayonets.
Gitstuckin.	Charge!
Ganon.	Quick march.
Givower.	Halt.
Ootyerpits.	Wakey-wakey'
Lowpoot. (for paratroops).	Geronimo!
Coinleft.	Left turn.
General	
Areyegan doonbye?	Are you contemplating a visit to the local pub, civic centre, home of your fiance, parish church, house of ill repute, social club, the cinema, etc., etc., etc.